Hollywood's Chinese Theatre

The Hand and Footprints of the Stars

from the Silents to "Star Trek"

by

...acey Endres and Robert Cushman

Pomegranate Press, Ltd.
Los Angeles   London
Printed in Korea

This is a Pomegranate Press, Ltd. book.

Pomegranate Press, Ltd.
PO Box 8261 Universal City, CA 91608-0261

Acknowledgments

We were greatly encouraged by the immediate enthusiasm for the project by the Mann Theatre Corporation, which had purchased the Chinese Theatre in 1973. The cooperation of Ted Mann, Chairman and Chief Executive Officer, plus the generous assistance of his Director of Marketing and Public Relations, William F. Hertz, and his administrative assistant, Mary Lyday, was always enthusiastic and whole-hearted.

For their various courtesies and cooperation, we wish to thank the following organizations and individuals who helped to make this book a reality:

Academy of Motion Picture Arts and Sciences' Center for Motion Picture Study, Margaret Herrick Library; Alan Berliner Photography; Bettmann Archive (UPI/Bettmann Newsphotos); Eddie Brandt's Saturday Matinee; Chapman's Picture Palace; Bruce Torrence/Hollywood Historical Collection; University of California, Los Angeles, Department of Special Collections; University of California, Los Angeles, Theater Arts Library; University of Southern California, Cinema-Television Library and Archives of Performing Arts; University of Wisconsin, Wisconsin Center for Film and Theater Research; Marc Wanamaker/Bison Archives;
and:

Rudy Behlmer, Richard Brian, Leroy Chen, Clarence and Eleanore Endres, Heidi Frieder, Bob Hope, Wyn Hope, DeForest Kelley, Walter Koenig, Tina McKenzie, Ben Martin, Arthur Marx, Nichelle Nichols, Frans Offermans, Howard Prouty, Charles "Buddy" Rogers, Ginger Rogers, Roy Rogers, Kathryn Leigh Scott, George Stevens, Jr., James Stewart, George Takei, and Elizabeth Taylor.

For Rudy,
Judith,
and
my parents,
with love, gratitude, and respect.

S.E.

To the memory of Mrs. Evelyn Spray, my extraordinary English teacher at Fort Wayne, Indiana South Side High School, who provided me with a solid foundation in the basics of writing, grammar, and composition;
And to the memory of Mary Pickford, a great star, a great actress, and a great human being, without whose inspiration, enthusiasm, and encouragement, I never would have become professionally involved with the world of film history in the first place.

R.C.

Foreword

When I was invited by Sid Grauman to place my hand and footprints in the forecourt of his beautiful Chinese Theatre on September 5, 1939, I couldn't have been more thrilled. I had just returned from a much needed vacation in Hawaii about three weeks before, and was finishing up some retakes at the studio.

I thought about how my prints would look in cement, for all time!—and wanted them to be smaller if I could manage it. I could do nothing about the size of my hands, but my footprints—those I could make smaller. My shoe size was about 5-1/2 and my mother Lela had a smaller size shoe than I: 4-1/2. So, I borrowed a pair of my mother's shoes and slipped my toes into them and stepped into the cement and made my prints!

I sure was glad when I could take off the "cement shoes" and put on my regular walking shoes again.

I am pleased to have this opportunity to share my memories of Hollywood's Chinese Theatre, and in these pages you'll read about the many celebrities represented in the forecourt throughout the theatre's glamorous sixty-five year history.

Ginger Rogers

The Footprint Ceremonies

Lives of great men all remind us
We can make our lives sublime,
And, departing, leave behind us
Footprints on the sands of time.
—Henry Wadsworth Longfellow

From the lyric poem "A Psalm of Life" (1838)

The idea of putting the footprints, hand-prints, and signatures of the stars in cement squares in the forecourt of the Chinese Theatre originated prior to its opening and has proven to be the single most effective, famous, and longest running publicity stunt in the history of the movies. There are many different accounts in print as to how the idea for the custom was born. Published versions of how the idea for the footprints originated include the following:

1) The most widely publicized version states that silent screen star Norma Talmadge accidentally stepped into some wet cement while visiting the construction site of the theatre and that Sid Grauman, witnessing the incident, was inspired with the idea. Variations of this account have Talmadge, Mary Pickford, and Douglas Fairbanks arriving in a car for a visit together, with Pickford inadvertently stepping in the wet cement.

2) Hollywood columnist Hedda Hopper stated that during the theatre's construction, Sid visited super star Mary Pickford at her studio bungalow on business. There was some wet cement in front of her bungalow, and a passer-by carelessly stepped in it. Seeing this incident, Sid got the idea, summoned Mary, whisked her over to the Chinese site, and had "America's Sweetheart" put her prints in wet cement. Another version of this story has Sid himself stepping into the wet cement outside Pickford's bungalow and telling Mary his idea and that he wanted her to be the first celebrity imprinted.

3) Mary Pickford stated that she had visited the Chinese construction site one afternoon and was returning home to Pickfair where a new cement driveway had just been poured. Her dog Zorro ran across the wet cement, leaving imprints, as Mary was getting out of her car. At first she was upset with the dog's unintentional piece of vandalism, but suddenly an idea clicked, and she called Sid, proposing that she and her husband, the extraordinarily popular screen star Douglas Fairbanks, install their prints in the Chinese forecourt and start a tradition. Mary said that she let Sid take credit for the idea since

he was the builder of the theatre and a good friend. A similar version of this story has Zorro running through the cement at the theatre's construction site itself.

4) Author Gary Carey offers another Pickford/Fairbanks variation which has Doug and Mary at their Rancho Zorro overseeing improvements they were making on the property. They were building an irrigation dam, and the cement was still wet; they bent down and pressed their hand prints in it and wrote their names. Having recently been to the Chinese site, one of them came up with the idea of stars placing their prints there.

5) Film historian Ronald Haver claims that the chief mason on the project, Jean W. Klossner, performed the centuries-old custom of placing his signature in the form of a hand print in the wet cement. When

The Chinese Theatre shortly before its opening on May 18, 1927. A 1984 Mann Theatres press release states, "An old Chinese Proverb says: 'To visit Los Angeles and not see the Chinese is like visiting China and not seeing the Great Wall.'"

Sid noticed the imprint, he questioned Klossner about the practice; and from that encounter, with input and advice from Klossner, Sid devised the footprints idea. Another version of this story has Klossner coming up with the idea himself and giving it to Sid.

6) Publicist Arthur S. Wenzel, who worked for Grauman for forty years, wrote to *Variety* in 1975: "...I recall walking with Sid when the Chinese was still incomplete. Sid suddenly slipped off a builder's plank into wet cement. Eyeing his own imprint, he shouted, 'Arthur, I am going to have all the stars recorded here.' That must have been in 1926."

7) Harry Hammond (Ham) Beall, another veteran Grauman publicist, who died in 1952, is "credited with originating" the footprints, according to his obituaries in the Los Angeles *Examiner*

and *Variety*. The information as to just *how* he supposedly did this is not supplied. Other obits say only that Hammond "promoted [the] footprinting of famous film stars" at the theatre.

8) Sid's own basic version of the story (told with several variations, as he was a notorious spinner of "tall tales") is that during construction, he accidentally stepped in newly smoothed wet cement. While a worker was bawling him out for ruining the slab, the idea suddenly hit him. He immediately called Douglas Fairbanks, Mary Pickford, and Norma Talmadge at their studios and, in a very agitated state, urged them to come immediately to the Chinese site with no explanation. Thinking he'd gone mad, they all appeared shortly thereafter, at which time Sid told them his idea and persuaded them to make their prints.

9) Grauman also said that he was punished as a child for marking some wet cement and that, ever after, he wanted to do it legally.

Of all the versions, Sid's own seems the least credible. Pickford, Fairbanks, and Talmadge, even though close friends and business associates of Sid, had extremely busy and demanding schedules; so it is hard to believe that these three stars could have dropped everything simultaneously on the spur of the moment in the middle of a working day and gone racing over to the theatre's construction site without even knowing why they were headed there. The true and exact story of the origin of the footprint idea may never be known: there are simply too many variations, and the participants in the mystery are now all deceased.

The selection of who is invited to be imprinted in the forecourt has been the decision of the theatre ownership since Sid Grauman's death. (Grauman himself made the decision during his lifetime.) Theatre management claimed it was a secret process, but the honor was usually accompanied by heavy overtones of publicity—often the new honoree had a motion picture to promote that just happened to be playing concurrently at the theatre. Still, many people agree with columnist Sidney Skolsky, who wrote in his December 8, 1961 Hollywood *Citizen-News* column: "I'd say that next to winning an Oscar the greatest tribute that can be shown a movie star is to have the outline of his hand and foot enshrined in concrete at Grauman's Chinese." In recent years, Ted Mann felt that his executives were perhaps overly careful about who was chosen to be honored but reasoned, "We've had offers....The remaining spaces are too important to waste. You need a star who will survive, and how many are there today?" As of this writing, there are still several blank, waiting-to-be-imprinted squares in the forecourt that have not yet been filled.

The Stars in the Forecourt

Mary Pickford and Douglas Fairbanks

Ceremony #1: April 30, 1927

The couple were husband and wife at the time of their ceremony. They wed in 1920 and divorced in 1936.

Silent screen stars Mary Pickford and Douglas Fairbanks posed for photographs during which they practiced making their imprints in a single square which was eventually smoothed over and used by Fairbanks on that day. Pickford placed her prints in a separate block two squares to the left of her

husband's. The square dividing them was later occupied with the imprints of another silent screen star, Norma Talmadge.

At the time of the ceremony the box-office was a decorative Chinese pagoda in the northeast corner of the forecourt. The squares of Pickford and Fairbanks graced the center of the open area directly in front of the theatre's main entrance doors and were easily viewable from the sidewalk. Today the box-office sits dead center at the forecourt's entrance along Hollywood Boulevard, and the canopy that runs from the box-office to the entrance shades and partially obstructs what was once the choicest area in the forecourt.

Pickford was a friend of the Grauman family, aside from being one of Sid's business partners. D.J. Grauman (Sid's father) himself bestowed the nickname "America's Sweetheart" on her in connection with the film *Tess of the Storm Country* (1914), which made Mary the most popular woman in the world.

Sid Grauman (left), Mary Pickford, and her husband Douglas Fairbanks.

Gloria Swanson

Ceremony #8: circa 1927

One of the most important and glamorous actresses of the 1920s, Gloria Swanson was a long-time friend of Sid Grauman. One of

his famous practical jokes was sending her—deftly made up—to see producer Jesse L. Lasky as an "unknown" hopeful looking for work. Lasky was one of the co-founders of Paramount where Swanson was then under contract. At the time, Gloria was a major star and drew an enormous weekly salary. Grauman hoped Lasky wouldn't recognize her and would try and sign her at $125 per week. Just as Sid had wished, Lasky didn't recognize the real Gloria Swanson under the makeup. However, he declined to hire this "unknown" girl at any price, saying she reminded him too much of somebody already in pictures!

Later, Swanson was away from Hollywood for a period of two years. She made a triumphant return on the occasion of the premiere of *Madame Sans-Gêne* (1925) at Sid's Million Dollar Theatre in downtown Los Angeles. When Gloria and her third husband, the Marquis Henri de la Falaise de la Coudraye, arrived by private train at the Los Angeles depot, they found all Hollywood turned out to welcome them.

In 1950, after years of relative inactivity in films, Swanson made a stunning impact portraying Norma Desmond, a faded silent screen star, in *Sunset Boulevard*. The film provided her with one of the most memorable lines of all time: "I *am* big. It's the *pictures* that got small." When Desmond first encounters Joe Gillis (William Holden), a down-on-his-luck hack writer, she orders him out of her mansion. He replies, "Next time I'll bring my autograph album along, or maybe a hunk of cement and ask for your footprints."

Gloria Swanson and Sid Grauman.

The Marx Brothers

Ceremony #22 February 17, 1933

They placed their prints in connection with the motion picture Duck Soup *(Paramount, 1933), in which they starred.*

As a joke, the four Marx Brothers and Sid Grauman paraded along Hollywood Boulevard that day dressed in Scottish kilts to protest the new trend in female fashions allowing women to wear slacks!

In his memoirs, writer Arthur Marx had the following to say about his father Groucho and his hand and footprint ceremony:

"'What do I want to do that for?' he'd say, whenever the Paramount Publicity Department brought up the subject. 'What good will it do me?'

"Informed that any publicity was good, Father replied, 'There are an awful lot of actors who have their footprints in there that can't get jobs any more. It's not doing them much good.'

"Under constant pressure, he finally consented, 'But only one foot!' he stipulated. 'If Paramount picks up our option, I'll give you the other foot.'"

Groucho called the Marx Brothers ceremony "a ritual that cemented our foothold in Hollywood...." He went on to recount that when Zeppo left the act, a local newspaper ran a photograph of what had originally been the four Marx Brothers at their Chinese Theatre ceremony, only then it looked as though just Groucho, Harpo, and Chico had placed their prints—Zeppo was gone! Groucho commented, "There was no more conclusive evidence that Zeppo was now a civilian than the neat

doctoring job of a Los Angeles tabloid. Zeppo was cut out of one of the pictures of our ritual in concrete at Grauman's and the background was shadowed in. Now we were three."

According to the family of cement artist Jean W. Klossner, Harpo decided it would be amusing to pummel the reporters in attendance with wet cement; and a cement-slinging contest ensued. (The Klossners do not elaborate as to how the reporters reacted to this idea.)

The Marx Brothers (Harpo [left], Groucho, Zeppo, and Chico) and Sid Grauman.

Jean Harlow

Ceremony #23: September 25, 1933

Ceremony #24: September 29, 1933

She placed her prints in connection with the motion pictures Dinner at Eight *and* Bombshell *(both Metro-Goldwyn-Mayer, 1933). Harlow's first square was never placed in the forecourt; one can only assume that it was planned to be located in the same location as her present square.*

One of the 1930s' greatest stars, Jean Harlow was revered world-wide as "the platinum blonde bombshell," an image that somewhat obscures her rightful claim to fame as a brilliant and scintillating comic actress.

Harlow placed her prints in a wet cement slab that had been wheeled on to the actual stage of the theatre—a result of Sid's first attempt to have a footprinting ceremony inside, before a live—and paying—audience. This attempt failed, as the cement dried too quickly. While it was being moved, one half dropped to the floor and smashed into bits in front of the audience.

Harlow was honored with another ceremony at the Chinese Theatre four days later. Unlike the first attempt to record her prints, Harlow's second ceremony took place outside in the forecourt of the theatre before an enthusiastic (and non-paying) crowd.

The family of cement artist Jean W. Klossner has a different account of this ceremony that is entertaining, but apocryphal. According to the Klossner family, Harlow arrived wearing sandals, shoes not appropriate to leave the desired prints. A search was made among the crowd to find her proper shoes. Klossner's own daughter

was present. A Hollywood High School student at the time, she doffed her saddle shoes, and Harlow made her impression in them. However, photographs of Harlow at both her ceremonies clearly show that her prints were made with high heels.

Jean Harlow at her second Chinese Theatre imprint ceremony.

Shirley Temple

Ceremony #26: March 14, 1935

She placed her prints in connection with the motion picture The Little Colonel *(Fox, 1935).*

Sid Grauman appeared as a guest on a "Lux Radio Theatre" broadcast of *A Star Is Born* in 1937 and had the following recollection about Shirley Temple, unquestionably the most popular child star in film history, and her footprint ceremony:

"When Shirley came to the theatre to leave her footprints she asked me if I'd mind if she took off her shoes and socks. I told her that we couldn't do that because she'd get her feet all full of concrete. As usual she had an answer ready. 'We can get some warm water and a towel and I'll wash them very carefully.' 'But why,' I asked, 'do you want to make your footprints in bare feet?' 'Mr. Grauman,' she said, 'I just want to be different.'"

Temple recalled in her memoirs: "For rising movie stars it was noblesse oblige to register hand and footprints in wet cement in the forecourt plaza of Grauman's Chinese.... A wall of gaping people pressed in to gawk at my investiture. At this moment of maximum exposure, out fell my first baby tooth, an incisor, right in the middle of my smile. Furtively, I spit it into my hand.

" 'Smile for the photographers,' Mother whispered, unaware. With lips pursed, I grinned. The cameras were all on my face.

"[Cement artist] Jean W. Klossner...was beside me in

his flowing robe and medieval beret and pointed to a square of glistening wet cement where I should place my foot.

"A-ha, the foot! Get all those cameras and eyes off my face and onto something else.

"'These shoes make my feet too big,' I mumbled behind my palm. 'Can I do it barefoot?'

"Slowly removing one shoe and sock, I wiggled the bare toes to catch camera attention, holding my face pointed down at all times."

Klossner recalled in 1953 that seven-year-old Shirley "...was so tiny, I had to help her write her own name."

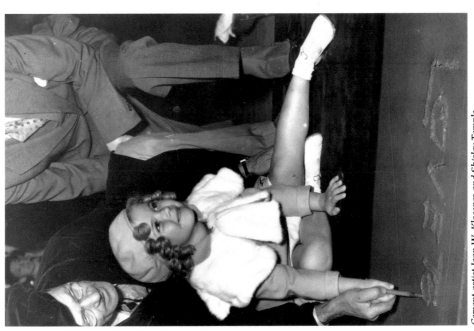

Cement artist Jean W. Klossner and Shirley Temple.

William Powell
and Myrna Loy

Ceremony #32: October 20, 1936

They placed their prints in connection with the motion picture Libeled Lady *(Metro-Goldwyn-Mayer, 1936).*

William Powell and Myrna Loy were renowned for being "The Perfect Mr. and Mrs. of the Screen." They had appeared together in five films at the time of their ceremony and would later co-star in an additional eight.

When Powell and Loy emerged from their limousine, a roar of laughter was heard from the crowd. Sid Grauman, who had stepped forward to greet them, couldn't figure out what was so funny until he glanced at their feet and cried, "Oh, Bill! Don't do this to me. This is a serious proposition!" Powell recalled his and Loy's ceremony during the filming of *Dancing in the Dark* (1949), part of which was set at the Chinese Theatre: "We had each put on a pair of those three-foot-long comedy shoes, something like the flippers swimmers wear. Sid went white when he saw them, but hastily pretended he knew it was a gag, and urged us to take them off so we could get on with the ceremony in our real shoes. We played it

straight and insisted the flippers were the only shoes we had, and solemnly told him that we'd worn them deliberately so we could make a bigger 'impression' than any he had in the forecourt. He began to protest that the slab of wet cement wasn't big enough to hold our imprints, when we finally got our [regular] shoes out of the car to go through with it. But not before we had a considerable

discussion during which we kept wriggling our flippers around.

"Since then there have been several funny stunts at the Chinese—John Barrymore allowed his profile to be recorded in the cement, Betty Grable her leg, and Monty Woolley his beard. But I think Myrna and I were the first to gag it up."

William Powell (left), Sid Grauman, and Myrna Loy.

Clark Gable and
W.S. Van Dyke II

Ceremony #33: January 20, 1937

They placed their prints in connection with the motion picture Love on the Run *(Metro-Goldwyn-Mayer, 1936); Gable starred, and Van Dyke directed.*

In 1936 Clark Gable was voted "The King of the Movies" in a public opinion poll. The title sums up Gable's supremacy in Hollywood to perfection.

Gable's Chinese Theatre appearance drew the largest crowd on record at the footprint ceremonies up to that time. His distinctive hair style was for his role in the motion picture *Parnell* (1937).

There is a brass border around Gable's square, which was added when the square was rededicated on February 11, 1976 in connection with the

Chinese Theatre premiere of *Gable and Lombard*, starring James Brolin and Jill Clayburgh.

Over the years, W.S. Van Dyke II directed several films that played the Chinese Theatre. MGM's first sound picture (synchronized sound effects and music with fragmentary non-synchronized dialogue), *White Shadows in the South Seas*, was a major turning point in Van Dyke's career and premiered there on August 3, 1928.

At the premiere Western star Tim McCoy spoke into the microphone and said the following to the crowd and radio audience: "I know we're going to see a great picture tonight, for I know the man who made it. He directed most of my best pictures, and I know how he works....You don't know who I'm talking about because his name wasn't even mentioned in the papers today....His name is W.S. Van Dyke, and you're going to hear a lot about this director from this night on. Mark my word!"

Van Dyke became one of the most important and successful directors at Metro-Goldwyn-Mayer studios from the late 1920s through the early 1940s, making such popular pictures as *Trader Horn* (1931), *Tarzan, the Ape Man* (1932), *The Thin Man* (1934), *Naughty Marietta* (1935), *San Francisco* (1936), and *Marie Antoinette* (1938).

Sid Grauman (left), W.S. Van Dyke II, Clark Gable, and cement artist Jean W. Klossner.

Fred Astaire

Ceremony #42: February 4, 1938

Fred Astaire is the most acclaimed dancer in motion picture history. He nearly single-handedly discovered and demonstrated that dance could be effectively and significantly integrated with plot in film. He admitted that his suave, bon-vivant, elegant, devil-may-care image belied his true personality: an absolute perfectionist and relentless taskmaster. He once said, "The only way I know to get a good show is to practice, sweat, rehearse and worry." And he loathed wearing "top hat, white tie, and tails."

Fred and his sister Adele began dancing lessons when they were children and over the years went from vaudeville to stardom in Broadway musicals. Adele married into the British aristocracy and chose to retire; so Fred decided to pursue a film career. RKO put him under contract and cast him opposite the vivacious Ginger Rogers in *Flying Down to Rio* (1933). They were a sensation and quickly became one of the most popular screen duos in the history of film, making a total of ten co-starring vehicles over the years. Later, when Rogers was footprinted at the Chinese Theatre on September 5, 1939, the spot selected for her was alongside Astaire. It could be said that the team has the most famous feet represented in the forecourt.

British actor Michael Crawford appeared in several motion pictures, including *Hello, Dolly!* (1969), and recounted in an April 29, 1990 Los Angeles *Times* article the following incident which took place on the morning of his final Los Angeles performance in the title role of the phenomenally successful stage musical, *The Phantom of the Opera*:

"Grauman's Chinese....The Hollywood premiere for *Hello, Dolly!* was held there. I'd never visited it as a tourist, so early last Christmas morning, I went with...[two] friends to...explore and compare all the footprints. I stood in Fred Astaire's and had my picture taken."

Fred Astaire (left) and cement artist Jean W. Klossner.

Judy Garland

Ceremony #50: October 10, 1939

She placed her prints in connection with the motion picture Babes in Arms *(Metro-Goldwyn-Mayer, 1939)*

Judy Garland has been called "the greatest entertainer of the 20th century." Her rich singing voice throbbed with passion and sensitivity, and she was also a fine actress and skilled dancer.

Her big turning point came in 1935 when she was signed by MGM. Garland was cast as Dorothy in *The Wizard of Oz* (1939) and in 1940 received a Special Academy Award "for her outstanding performance as a screen juvenile during the past year."

Garland was assisted at her footprint ceremony by co-star Mickey Rooney. She was wearing her first formal evening gown and later joked that Rooney made a less-than-dignified entrance with her when he whispered in her ear, "Walk around the cement, Jootes, not through it!" ("Jootes" was Mickey's pet name for "Judy.") Garland recalled in 1943:

"What promised to be the most exciting night of my life turned out to be the most embarrassing. It was the premiere of *Babes in Arms*, and the night I placed my hand and foot prints in the forecourt of the Chinese Theatre. I wanted to look more glamorous than ever before. Now I must confess I had the habit of biting my fingernails. I was just sick that I couldn't have long, glittering fingertips. But the manicurist fixed that. She gave me false nails. After I placed my hands in the cement

we went inside to see the picture. Suddenly I thought creeping paralysis had set in, beginning at my fingertips. I was in a cold sweat before we left the theatre—then I realized some of the cement had crept under my nails and hardened. The next day I had to have my 'glamour' chipped off."

Garland's mother also attended the event and straightened out a letter in her daughter's signature after the ceremony.

Mickey Rooney (left), Judy Garland, and her mother Ethel Gumm.

John Barrymore

Ceremony #54: September 5, 1940

He placed his prints in connection with the motion picture The Great Profile *(20th Century-Fox, 1940).*

The legendary John Barrymore, "The Great Profile," was one of the consummate actors of the 20th century. At his footprint ceremony, Barrymore misspelled his name in his first attempt at writing his signature ("Jon Barrymore"). The cement had to be smoothed over, and he got it right on the second try.

Sid Grauman told news reporters before the ceremony that photographs would be taken of Barrymore merely placing his cheek

next to the cement and added that the actual profile was to be made later from a plaster cast.

A cloth was spread over the wet concrete to protect Barrymore's attire, and he went ahead with the publicity stunt but imprinted his actual profile, without any cast. (Accounts of Grauman's taking it upon himself to sneak up and push Barrymore's face into the cement without forewarning him are questionable.) The actor commented, "I feel like the face on the barroom floor."

Barrymore was none too happy. His muffled obscenities while he was deep in the goo could not be recounted in print by the attending news media. A photograph from one of the local Los Angeles papers covering the event shows a disgruntled Barrymore digging wet cement out of his left ear with his index finger.

Sid drew a few hair strands in the damp concrete while actress Mary Beth Hughes helped clean Barrymore's face with a towel supplied by a theatre attendant. When his limousine drove away, poor John Barrymore was still dabbing his cemented left eye with his handkerchief.

Sid Grauman pushes John Barrymore's face into the cement.

Henry Fonda, Rita Hayworth, Charles Laughton, Edward G. Robinson, and Charles Boyer

Ceremony #66: July 24, 1942

They placed their prints in connection with the motion picture Tales of Manhattan *(20th Century-Fox, 1942).*

The stars of *Tales of Manhattan* set a forecourt record that stands to this day: Five stars, five individual squares imprinted on the same day.

The film was a modern story consisting of five separate sequences which are related by a connecting link—a gentleman's full-dress tail coat with a curse on it. At first, the garment is worn by an actor (Boyer) who is shot by the husband of the woman (Hayworth) with whom he has been having an affair. It is next passed along to a bridegroom (Fonda), a composer (Laughton), and a hobo (Robinson). It is finally thrown out of an airplane and used to dress a farmer's scarecrow.

Publicity for the picture boasted "the largest assembly of stars in Hollywood." Other prominent players in the film included Ginger Rogers (who had placed her footprints at the Chinese Theatre on September 5, 1939),

Paul Robeson, Ethel Waters, and Eddie "Rochester" Anderson. *Tales of Manhattan* had its world premiere at the Chinese Theatre on August 5. All proceeds from the premiere were donated to World War II charities.

At the end of 1948, Hayworth became romantically involved with the man who would become her third husband, Prince Aly Khan. She had recently divorced Orson Welles and became the target of harsh criticism because the prince was a married man. Their romance and eventual marriage on the French Riviera the following May created world-

wide controversy.

During this period Sid Grauman was asked to remove Rita's square from the Chinese Theatre forecourt. He refused.

Charles Boyer (left), Sid Grauman, Charles Laughton, Henry Fonda, Edward G. Robinson, and Rita Hayworth.

Bob Hope and Dorothy Lamour

Ceremony #67: February 5, 1943

They placed their prints in connection with the motion picture They Got Me Covered *(RKO, 1943).*

Comedian Bob Hope has combined careers in film, radio, and television. He has been called the "quintessential American comic" and during the past thirty years has graduated to the status of cultural icon. His frequent co-star, Dorothy Lamour, made the sarong her world-famous trademark, becoming Hollywood's number one make-believe South Seas heroine during the 1930s and 1940s. The pictures *The Jungle Princess* (1936) and *The Hurricane* (1937) quickly established Lamour's image and made her an important star. One of her colorful sarongs now resides in the permanent collection of the Smithsonian Institution in Washington, D.C.

In 1940 the two teamed with Bing Crosby (who had already been footprinted at the Chinese Theatre on April 8, 1936) for *Road to Singapore*. Subsequent "Road" pictures led to *Zanzibar* (1941), *Morocco* (1942), *Utopia* (1946), *Rio* (1947), *Bali* (1952), and *Hong Kong* (1962).

Hope told the authors, "...from the way Lamour is

holding me, it looks like I'm drunk!"

Hope was the master of ceremonies at the 18th annual Academy Awards Presentation held at the Chinese Theatre on March 7, 1946 and made reference to his imprint ceremony in his opening monologue, saying, "I don't mind them having my nose print but they had a lot of nerve putting it between Lassie's paw and where Trigger sat down!" (It was a good joke, but Lassie is not represented in the forecourt, and Trigger still had more than three years to wait before his ceremony.)

Dorothy Lamour, Bob Hope, and cement artist Jean W. Klossner.

Betty Grable

Ceremony #68: February 15, 1943

She placed her prints in connection with the motion picture Coney Island *(20th Century-Fox, 1943).*

The day of her ceremony found pin-up girl and motion picture box-office champion Betty Grable assisted by Marine Sergeant B.L. Duckett, Naval Gunner's Mate third class J.O. Buchanan, and Army Sergeant Albert Woas. They had volunteered their services as a "thank you" for Grable's many personal appearances at military establishments throughout the U.S. during World War II.

Newspaper accounts reported that it took an hour and a half to get Grable's leg imprint (Grable was world-famous for her "million dollar legs") and that she wasn't wearing stockings. The initial plan was for Buchanan to grasp Grable around the shoulders, Duckett to hold her gently at the waist, and Woas to clasp her at the hips. Sounds easy, doesn't it? It wasn't.

The problem was that the skirt Betty wore on the occasion kept hiking up alarmingly. (Her mother had suggested her daughter wear a bathing suit; but Grable opted for a dress, saying it was more modest.) The servicemen were forced to try again. They regrouped, but Grable's skirt continued to prove a problem, and the proceedings stopped once again.

Trying new leverage, the service men lifted Grable into the air and almost dropped her! Betty let out a scream as her three assistants caught her in time and gently placed her anatomy into the concrete. She exclaimed, "Ooooh, it's cold!" and was a good sport while she waited for the concrete to set up.

Each serviceman wrote the initials of his branch of the service in the square. When they finished, Betty shook hands with her helpers and hurried home to see if she could remove the wet cement from her skirt before it set. As she departed, Gunner's Mate Buchanan said, "I think that girl was a little nervous. She didn't seem exactly comfortable. I did my best to put her at her ease."

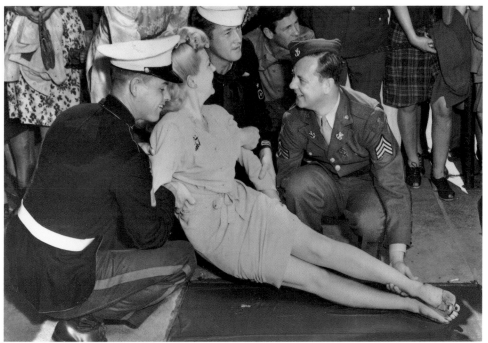

Sergeant B.L. Duckett (left), Betty Grable, Gunner's Mate third class J.O. Buchanan, and Sergeant Albert Woas.

Humphrey Bogart

Ceremony #77: August 21, 1946

He placed his prints in connection with the motion picture The Big Sleep *(Warner Bros., 1946).*

Humphrey Bogart's screen image of iron-willed toughness, cynicism, brutal honesty, bluntness, and sometime arrogance was tempered with a brooding inner pain and emotionalism which his characters tried to suppress.

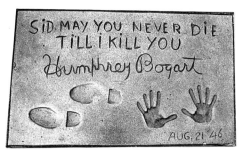

The inscription in his square ("Sid—May You Never Die Till I Kill You") kidded Bogart's tough-guy image as a screen gangster. Earlier in his career he had been known as the screen's "No. 1 Bad Boy." Warner Bros., impressed by the feminine reaction to Bogart's performance in *Dark Victory* (1939), helped him break out of that early stereotype; and he became a successful leading man with considerable romantic appeal.

Bogart, shooting *Dead Reckoning* (1947), worked until the late afternoon on the day of his ceremony. He paused to put on his "lucky" shoes—those he wore in *Casablanca* (1942) and *The Big Sleep*—before rushing over to the theatre.

In April 1992 *Casablanca* celebrated its fiftieth anniversary, and the Chinese Theatre was chosen as the Los Angeles site to screen the film. Forty-eight years before, on March 2, 1944, *Casablanca* had won the Best Picture, Direction, and Writing (Screenplay) Oscars at the 16th annual Academy Awards Presentation held at the Chinese Theatre. It was the first time the Oscar ceremony took place there.

In 1953 Bogart's wife, Lauren Bacall, was asked to make her prints in connection with *How To Marry a Millionaire*. Bogart told writer Joe Hyams, "It used to be an honor—it was at least back in 1946 when I did it." Bogart asked his wife, "Why don't you refuse?" Bacall, who later recalled her husband as "loving a chance to puncture Hollywood's ego," politely declined the theatre's offer, and the studio (20th Century-Fox) had to cancel the ceremony.

Humphrey Bogart, Sid Grauman (obscured), and Lauren Bacall (Mrs. Humphrey Bogart).

James Stewart

Ceremony #81: February 13, 1948

He placed his prints in connection with the motion picture Call Northside 777 *(20th Century-Fox, 1948).*

As a tall, rather gawky youth, a fresh-faced idealist with a slow, hesitant drawl—sometimes bordering on a stammer—Jimmy Stewart first endeared himself to American audiences in the late 1930s and has enjoyed a career as a great star over the decades.

Unlike his friend, actor Gary Cooper, (who was footprinted at the Chinese Theatre on August 13, 1943), Stewart was not the least bit hesitant about his ceremony being held on Friday the 13th. Photographs of the event show Stewart holding a black cat—it was on a leash—while posing underneath an opened step-ladder.

In a letter to the authors, Stewart recalled, "I remember that in the footprint ceremony at Grauman's Chinese, I misspelled my first name when I wrote it in the concrete and they had to smooth it over and I tried again."

Archie Henderson, a popcorn salesclerk in the theatre's outdoor snack stand, said in 1985, "People from all over the world come to gawk [at Stewart's footprints].

Only yesterday, a middle-aged woman from London curtsied to them. But that was mild compared to what a lady did a couple of months ago. She was so moved when she saw his handprints that she kept coming back every afternoon with a bucket filled with soap and water. She scrubbed like mad. 'I want Jimmy to always be clean,' she kept explaining."

In 1985 Stewart received an Honorary Academy Award "for his fifty years of memorable performances. [And] For his high ideals both on and off the screen. With the respect and affection of his colleagues."

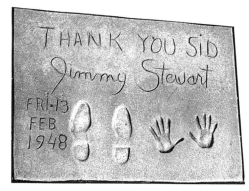

James Stewart.

Roy Rogers and Trigger

Ceremony #84: April 21, 1949

In 1943 Roy Rogers was dubbed "King of the Cowboys," a title to which he laid a rightful claim through another eight years of constant filmmaking and an additional six years and over 100 episodes of television's "The Roy Rogers Show" (1951-1957). Trigger, Rogers' golden palomino, appeared with Rogers in all of his nearly ninety starring film vehicles (1938-1951), as well as in all the episodes of "The Roy Rogers Show." Rogers once commented, "I'm the only cowboy in the business, I think, that started and made all my pictures with one horse."

Trigger's trainer, Glenn Randall, said, "He was a very exceptional horse. The title he had of 'The Smartest Horse in the Movies' absolutely fit. He was almost like a human; you could talk to him. He could do forty things by word cue." In addition to his responses to word commands, Trigger could perform fifty more tricks when given non-verbal cues.

He was originally owned by the Hudkins Rental Stable in Hollywood and named Golden Cloud. His first known screen role was as the steed of Maid Marian (played by Olivia de Havilland) in *The Adventures of Robin Hood* (1938). Rogers found Trigger while trying out horses immediately after he signed his first contract with Republic Pictures. At first the idea was to rent Trigger, but Rogers decided to purchase the animal and negotiated a sale in the amount of $2,500.

Rogers' long-time friend and "sidekick" in pictures in the late 1940s and early 1950s and on television, Pat

Brady, was present at the footprint ceremony. He congratulated his pal, saying "You've just reached the Hollywood pinnacle. Cowboys aren't usually invited to join the ranks of the all-time movie greats, you know."

Rogers shared his feelings about the event in a letter to the authors: "It was one of the highlights of my career. I enjoyed meeting Sid Grauman and inspecting all of the other stars' prints represented in the foyer. With my footprints there, I feel honored to be among so many great people, and I feel Trigger feels the same way."

(Left to right) Dale Evans (Mrs. Roy Rogers, kneeling), Pat Brady (standing directly behind her), Trigger , Rogers (kneeling), and cement artist Jean W. Klossner (far right).

John Wayne

Ceremony #90: January 25, 1950

He placed his prints in connection with the motion picture Sands of Iwo Jima *(Republic, 1949).*

A heroic figure, John Wayne created a unique and unforgettable persona as a leather-tough, two-fisted archetypal Westerner. He varied his roles, however, by often playing military men and even occasionally an actual civilian. In 1967 *Time* magazine called him "the greatest moneymaker in film history," his movies having grossed nearly $400,000,000 at that time. (That figure was revised to $700,000,000 in 1979.)

As a boy he had an Airedale dog named Duke, and somehow that name was transferred to Wayne as a permanent nickname. He got his first movie work at Fox studios as a laborer, prop man, and sometime set dresser. Eventually he began doing stunts and bits.

Wayne struck up a friendship with director John Ford, who recommended him to Raoul Walsh for the lead in Walsh's upcoming Western epic *The Big Trail* (1930), a breakthrough for Wayne and his first starring role.

Wayne spent the next eight years in "B" pictures, primarily at Republic in Westerns, and finally achieved full-fledged stardom in John Ford's *Stagecoach* (1939). He gained steady momentum during the 1940's, appearing in such popular films as *Fort Apache, Red River* (both 1948), and *She Wore a Yellow Ribbon* (1949).

Wayne was assisted at his footprint ceremony by several members of the U.S. Marine Corps, all of whom were

stationed at Iwo Jima, the site of a Japanese air base during World War II and an island taken at a great cost by U.S. forces in 1945. The sand used to mix Wayne's cement was literally the "Sands of Iwo Jima" and was shipped from the island to the theatre in two 100-pound sacks for the occasion.

Wayne's was the last ceremony at which Sid Grauman officiated. Grauman died on March 5, 1950. Mann Theatre Corporation reports that the imprints of Marilyn Monroe and John Wayne are the most photographed squares in the forecourt.

(Kneeling, left) Private Inga Boberg, John Wayne, Sid Grauman, and cement artist Jean W. Klossner (standing, right). (Standing, left) Major Gordon West, Lieutenant Colonel C.A. Youngdale, and Colonel J.O. Brauer.

Bette Davis

Ceremony #92: November 6, 1950

She placed her prints in connection with the motion picture All about Eve *(20th Century-Fox, 1950).*

At her footprint ceremony Bette Davis jokingly told the crowd, "It's too bad there's no way to imprint my poached-egg eyes here." She possessed a striking presence rather than conventional beauty, coupled with flamboyant mannerisms and a distinctive speaking style.

Actor George Arliss specifically requested Davis for *The Man Who Played God* (1932) at Warner Bros., and the studio placed her under long-term contact.

In 1938 Warners began putting her in only first-rate productions. As a result, Davis became the most acclaimed actress in Hollywood for many years and was called "The Fourth Warner Brother."

In 1942 Davis helped organize the Hollywood Canteen for World War II servicemen, which was a place in Hollywood for them to be entertained by and socialize with the stars. On the day of her footprint ceremony she was assisted by Canteen Marine Corps veterans Staff Sergeant Jack Spencer and Technical Sergeant Bert R. Nave as a tribute to her work as president of that organization. Davis wrote in 1987, "There are few accomplishments in my life that I am sincerely proud of. The Hollywood Canteen is one of them."

Ironically, Davis almost did not play the role of actress Margo Channing in *All About Eve*. Claudette Colbert was

originally cast in the part, but shortly before the picture was slated to begin she ruptured a disc as the result of playing a scene in *Three Came Home* (1950), and it became necessary to replace her. 20th Century-Fox studio head Darryl F. Zanuck personally called Davis, told her about the crisis, and sent the script to her. She read it and eagerly accepted.

Staff Sergeant Jack Spencer (left), Bette Davis, and Technical Sergeant Bert R. Nave.

Cary Grant

Ceremony #94: July 16, 1951

He placed his prints in connection with the motion picture People Will Talk *(20th Century-Fox, 1951).*

Cary Grant's ability to delight audiences has proved timeless. *The Awful Truth* (1937) made Grant a star of the first order; and subsequent pictures such as *Bringing Up Baby* (1938), *His Girl Friday*, and *The Philadelphia Story* (both 1940), established him as the foremost male player of sophisticated and screwball comedy.

Southern California tourist Georgia Douglas just happened to be visiting the Chinese Theatre with her husband on the day of Cary Grant's ceremony and recalled: "[We] noticed a crowd gathering to await the arrival of a motion picture star who was scheduled to leave an identifying mark in the square of wet cement. In a short time, a big black car drove up and Cary Grant emerged. He was most gracious to the public, shaking hands, joking and standing still while we snapped pictures with our tourist-type cameras. A platform about three inches high had been placed near the wet cement, and he knelt on it, leaned over and left an impression of his hands. An attendant stood by with a basin of water and towel, and after cleaning his hands, he again talked and laughed with the people.

"A short time before this, we had occasion to see another popular star, but his attitude was so cold and unfriendly we never again went to see a movie in which he played an important part.

"Mr. Grant was so congenial and friendly we felt we were lucky to have had the pleasure of watching and talking to him."

In the early 1950s Grant had a few mediocre vehicles and contemplated retirement. Alfred Hitchcock came to the rescue and gave the actor's career a much-needed rejuvenation with the successful *To Catch a Thief* (1955).

In 1970 Grant received an Honorary Academy Award "for his unique mastery of the art of screen acting with the respect and affection of his colleagues."

Cary Grant.

Jane Russell and Marilyn Monroe

Ceremony #104: June 26, 1953

They placed their prints in connection with the motion picture Gentlemen Prefer Blondes *(20th Century-Fox, 1953).*

Jane Russell recalled the occasion when she and Marilyn Monroe made their imprints at the Chinese Theatre in her memoirs:

"We were both wearing light, summery dresses and high heels as we posed, arms linked together, for the photographers. We were thrilled beyond words.... Always one for personal comfort, I was wearing my usual big shoes, so no aspiring actress will have any trouble whatsoever getting her feet into my footprints!"

Marilyn felt that she and Jane Russell should leave imprints other than those of their hands and feet, since the prints were to reflect your public personality: "I suggested that Jane lean over the wet cement and that I sit down in it and we could leave our prints that way, but my idea was vetoed. After that I suggested that Grauman's use a diamond to dot the 'i' in the 'Marilyn' I scratched in the wet concrete. They finally compromised on dotting it with a rhinestone, but some sightseer chiselled that rhinestone out."

The diamond idea was a reference to her hit song, "Diamonds Are a Girl's Best Friend," from the film.

Her friend, columnist Sidney Skolsky, wrote shortly after her death: "I read how Marilyn had looked longingly many times at the footprints—especially those of Jean Harlow's. She wished and hoped that someday her footprints would be here. I read that she waited two days and two nights for her footprints to dry—and the wooden fence [placed around the wet prints to protect them]

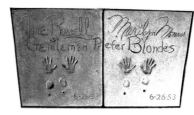

taken down. The second night, about two a.m., Marilyn got out of her brass bed, walked from her apartment [near the Chinese Theatre], and, with no one watching her, she stood in her footprints—alone. It was like hearing all the applause in the world."

Marilyn later confessed that the ceremony made her feel "anything's possible."

Marilyn Monroe (left) and Jane Russell.

Elizabeth Taylor, Rock Hudson, and George Stevens

Ceremony #113: September 26, 1956

They placed their prints in connection with the motion picture Giant *(Warner Bros., 1956); Taylor and Hudson starred; Stevens produced and directed.*

George Stevens, a meticulous craftsman, brought his special touch to dramas, comedies, Westerns, adventures, and even musicals with equal success. His son, George Stevens, Jr., who in 1967 became the founding director of the American Film Institute, shared his memories of the Taylor/Hudson/Stevens ceremony in a letter to the authors:

"The only recollection I have is that Elizabeth Taylor who, along with Rock Hudson and my father, was part of the program, arrived, as was her custom, a little bit late and the cement was drying and there was some question as to whether they were going to be able to remove their hands and feet from the rapidly congealing (is that what cement does?) cement."

Taylor told the authors, "I was twenty-four years of age at the time and was absolutely thrilled to be joining such a select group of personalities."

When *Giant* premiered at the Chinese Theatre on October 18, Hudson's wife Phyllis and two of his friends

were finishing work on a home movie detailing the events of Rock's footprint ceremony and *Giant's* east and west coast premieres in order to surprise Hudson on his birthday a few weeks later. The movie opens with Elizabeth Taylor pounding on his shoes to plant them deeper in the wet cement.

Hudson was delighted with the film and exclaimed, "This is terrific. How'd you guys do this? I never saw a thing!" He was nearsighted and in true movie star fashion at the time, never wore his glasses in public.

Theatre chain executives Edwin F. Zabell (kneeling left) and Frank H. Ricketson, Jr. with George Stevens (both standing); Elizabeth Taylor and Rock Hudson.

Doris Day

Ceremony #117: January 19, 1961

Actress Doris Day was and is natural, congenial, and ebullient. One fan said, "She looks as if she drinks a pint of liquid sunshine every day."

At sixteen she joined Barney Rapp's band in Cincinnati as lead singer; he changed her name from Doris Mary Anne von Kappelhoff to Doris Day when she had a hit with the song "Day after Day." She next had stints with the Bob Crosby and Les Brown bands.

In Los Angeles she was down on her luck and ready to return to Cincinnati when she was cast in *Romance on the High Seas* (1948) at Warner Bros. Day was an immediate hit. During her early Hollywood career she usually appeared in sprightly musicals but alternated with occasional dramatic roles, including *Love Me or Leave Me* (1955) and *The Man Who Knew Too Much* (1956). Day sang "Whatever Will Be, Will Be" ("Que Sera, Sera") in

the latter, and the song became her trademark. She achieved even greater popularity in the comedy *Pillow Talk* (1959), the first of three pictures opposite Rock Hudson.

George Gibson, who had staged the footprint ceremonies for three decades, said the Day event was "the biggest turnout since Sid Grauman 'accidentally' started this event back in 1927. Clark Gable in 1937 drew the biggest crowd until today, but Doris Day far outstripped that gathering." (Note: Other ceremonies since Gable that have been heavily attended by fans and members of the news media have claimed "record crowds," as well.)

Doris told the excited onlookers, "I can remember the time I walked around here, admiring other footprints but never dreaming I would be invited to be a part in such a ceremony."

When it was pointed out to Day that her inscribed "Jan" date looked more like "June," she hastily grabbed the trowel, smoothed the cement over, and began again. "I must be correct," she laughed. Doris was also given a "Star of Stars" award that day by the Hollywood Chamber of Commerce as being "Hollywood's foremost star" based on recent box-office grosses.

Carl H. Anderson, president of the Hollywood Chamber of Commerce (kneeling, left), Doris Day, and theatre chain executive Roy Evans.

Sophia Loren

Ceremony #120: July 26, 1962

She placed her prints in connection with the motion picture Boccaccio '70 *(Embassy International, 1962).*

Voluptuous Sophia Loren is the most popular star ever produced in the history of Italian cinema. Loren, accompanied by her husband, producer Carlo Ponti, flew in from Rome on the morning of July 26 for a one-day stay in Hollywood. The first scheduled stop on her itinerary was at the Chinese Theatre, where she placed her prints.

As she stood in the cement, Loren wiggled her hips back and forth in order to make a deeper impression in the wet concrete.

Newsmen noticed that Loren did not remove her wedding ring from her right hand nor a huge sapphire and diamond ring from her left when she plunged her hands into the cement.

She said her mother told her "to make one fingerprint in the cement for her. She couldn't believe I was going to have my feet and hands in the cement. She asked me if they would be there for eternity and I told her they would."

That evening the Pontis attended a dinner party in her honor at the Beverly Hills Hotel. Loren had not attended the 34th annual Academy Awards Presentation held on

April 9, 1962 when she was announced the winner of the Best Actress Oscar for her performance in *Two Women* (1960, a.k.a. *La Ciociara*). She was the first performer in a foreign-language film to be nominated for an Academy Award.

At the party at the Beverly Hills Hotel following her Chinese Theatre ceremony, Loren finally picked up her officially inscribed prize.

Sophia Loren.

Star Wars

Ceremony #143: August 3, 1977

See-Threepio/Anthony Daniels, Artoo-Detoo, and Lord Darth Vader placed their prints (in that order) in connection with the motion picture Star Wars *(20th Century-Fox, 1977).*

In early 1977 advance posters for *Star Wars* announced that the picture was "Coming To Your Galaxy This Summer." The film starred Mark Hamill, Harrison Ford, Carrie Fisher, and Alec Guinness; and when it opened on May 25 it quite literally took the world by storm. The picture was brilliantly imaginative; and its events and characters—Luke Skywalker, Han Solo, Princess Leia Organa, Ben (Obi-Wan) Kenobi, arch villain Darth Vader (the Dark Lord of the Sith), Chewbacca the Wookie, and the robots See-Threepio and Artoo-Detoo—almost immediately became a part of our contemporary mythology.

The footprint ceremony set the theatre's all-time attendance record—a crowd of 8,000 turned up for the event! The occasion was also another "first" for the theatre in that the film officially re-premiered that same day and moved back into the house for a resumed regular run. The picture had originally opened on May 25, 1977, at the Chinese Theatre, the Avco Center Cinema in Westwood, and Plitt's City Center Cinema in Orange.

Just as the eager spectators had hoped, Darth Vader was properly menacing, See-Threepio/Anthony Daniels delivered an enthusiastic thank you speech, and little Artoo-Detoo made his customary whistles, sighs, and beeps, much to the crowd's delight.

David Prowse, assisted by the voice of James Earl Jones, portrayed Lord Darth Vader; and Kenny Baker portrayed

Artoo-Detoo in the three *Star Wars* films. But of all the performers in the trilogy, only Anthony Daniels, in costume as See-Threepio, signed his name in the cement during the ceremony in the Chinese Theatre forecourt. Shortly after, Daniels commented, "Compared to the stars that are there, I am a bit embarrassed that I am there at all."

Star Wars (1977) character See-Threepio with unidentified persons.

Donald Duck and Clarence "Ducky" Nash

Ceremony #150: May 21, 1984

They placed their prints in celebration of the fiftieth anniversary of Donald's creation.

In terms of the total number of his screen, television, and comic book appearances, Donald Duck is the most prolific animated character in the history of the Walt Disney studios. His popularity is immense and challenges even that of Mickey Mouse, the "king of the lot."

For fifty years, only one man did the voice of Donald Duck. He was Clarence "Ducky" Nash, who joined the Disney organization in December 1933.

Nash was delighted when he heard early in 1984 that "Donald will be putting his feet in wet cement someplace." Donald's long-time girlfriend, Daisy Duck, was on hand for the footprint ceremony, which was only one of many celebrations during the year-long birthday festivities for Donald Duck's fiftieth anniversary.

That same year the world's best-known fowl was saluted at the 56th annual Academy Awards Presentation, the Indianapolis 500 Parade, and the Kentucky Derby. He also received a star on the Hollywood Walk of Fame. Los Angeles Mayor Tom Bradley issued a proclamation commemorating Donald's first screen appearance fifty years before, and June 9 was officially declared "Donald Duck Day" in Los Angeles. His career was the subject of an hour-long CBS television special, a four-week retrospective of his work in New York City, as well as an exhibition of Donald Duck animation art.

The Disney company was pleased. Disney executive Jack Lindquist, said, "Donald is a character very much into one-upmanship, so we wanted him to have one-up on Mickey Mouse, whose fiftieth birthday [in 1978] was a national event."

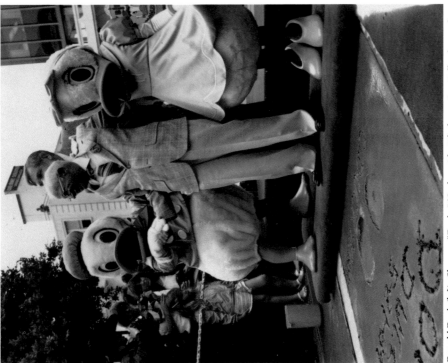

Donald Duck (left), Clarence "Ducky" Nash, unidentified man (partially obscured), and Daisy Duck.

Eddie Murphy and Hollywood's 100th Anniversary

Ceremony #153: May 14, 1987

Murphy placed his prints in connection with the motion picture Beverly Hills Cop II *(Paramount, 1987). He starred and co-wrote the story. His ceremony also took place on the same day that the Chinese Theatre celebrated the 100th anniversary of Hollywood. The city received an honorary plaque.*

Since 1982 comic actor Eddie Murphy has been among the most popular stars in the film medium. In 1988 his films were reported to have grossed in excess of one billion dollars, a first for a black performer. It was estimated that 5,000 people attended the footprinting event.

Of all the major studios that were located in the section of Los Angeles known as Hollywood, today only Paramount, Eddie Murphy's home studio, remains; but Hollywood is still synonymous the world over with the American motion picture industry, along with the excitement, luxury, glamour, and celebrity which are immediately associated with the movies.

Several historical sites and landmarks remain in Hollywood, and looking down on them is perhaps the most famous icon of them all—the Hollywood sign, which was most recently restored in 1978 and presides over the

community in its fifty-foot-high/270-foot-wide glory.

In 1928 Sid Grauman wrote an article in which he discussed the growth of the Hollywood community and its famous theatres. The showman said in part:

"...My attention was directed to Hollywood in the first place as an unexploited field for the showman....It has...the supreme advantage of being the world's film center, despite many attempts to shear it of this glory by other ambitious communities and cities...."

Eddie Murphy (kneeling, center), unidentified man, and William F. Hertz, director of marketing and public relations for Mann Theatres (kneeling, right).

Star Trek

The Twenty-fifth Anniversary (1966-1991) and its creator Gene Roddenberry, and featured players William Shatner, Leonard Nimoy, DeForest Kelley, James Doohan, Walter Koenig, Nichelle Nichols, and George Takei

Ceremony #154: December 5, 1991

The players placed their prints in connection with the motion picture Star Trek VI: The Undiscovered Country (Paramount, 1991). Nimoy was also the executive producer and co-wrote the story. The television series and its creator received an honorary plaque.

The original "Star Trek" (1966-1991) cast set a new Chinese Theatre record: seven stars, one imprinted square.

Four of the stars spoke with the authors. Kelley expressed delight when recalling the ceremony, admitting, "The seven of us are there only through the grace of 'Star Trek.'"

Koenig admitted "I hadn't done anything like that since I was eleven years old and wrote the name of my local neighborhood gang, the 'Payson Avenue Braves,' in fresh cement."

Nichols said, "It was so meaningful to me on a very personal level, because many years ago, I stood there with my father. He told me then, 'Baby, some day your name will be here!'"

Takei confided, "Before the ceremony Paramount instructed all seven of us that we were strictly forbidden to put down any imprints save our signatures. I am the only Los Angeles native in the group and I know how this

ceremony is supposed to be done! Everyone else had written their signatures, complying with the request; but when my turn came I signed my name and placed a handprint. What were they [Paramount] going to do, after all? Bill Shatner said, 'Look at that! George placed his handprint!' So everyone else got back down and added their hand imprints."

Left to right: Walter Koenig, William Shatner, Leonard Nimoy, DeForest Kelley, and James Doohan. Nichelle Nichols (center) embraces George Takei.

The Squares That Vanished

Over the years, rumors have persisted of theatre officials moving quietly into the forecourt under the dark of night to take away older squares and place them in storage, thereby making room for the inclusion of current celebrities. These stories are absolutely untrue, although there are four squares originally in the forecourt that have been removed under other circumstances.

In early 1928 Charles Chaplin placed his prints in connection with his motion picture *The Circus* (1928). Chaplin was at the height of his fame and popularity when the ceremony took place. As a result of his four marriages, three divorces, a paternity suit in the 1940s (in which he was found innocent), and his alleged "Communist sympathies," Chaplin became a controversial figure. At some point during the Senator Joseph McCarthy-inspired investigations in the early 1950s, the hate campaign directed at Charlie resulted in his square being quietly removed or simply cemented over.

On October 11, 1938 Jean Hersholt placed his prints, and the footprints of the Dionne Quintuplets, in connection with the motion picture *Five of a Kind* (1938). The square was not made by cement artist Jean W. Klossner. The ceremony took place during one of Klossner's and Sid Grauman's disagreements, and Grauman hired another man to prepare the cement. The square started to deteriorate badly in a matter of weeks and eventually had to be removed. Today the large space is occupied by the two squares of Dorothy Lamour and Bob Hope. Hersholt was honored with another ceremony at the Chinese Theatre, when in 1949 he again recorded his hand and footprints.

On October 18, 1938 Mickey Rooney placed his prints in connection with the motion picture *Stablemates* (1938). Like the Dionne/Hersholt square, Rooney's deteriorated and eventually crumbled into bits, although forty-eight years went by before it was removed. Mann Theatres officials explained the situation to Rooney, who graciously obliged with another hand and footprint ceremony in 1986. Today the original spot is occupied by Rooney's second square.

On August 30, 1954 Hollywood newcomer Edmund Purdom placed his prints in connection with the motion picture *The Egyptian* (1954), in which he starred. Almost immediately, controversy ensued over Purdom's inclusion in the forecourt. Hedda Hopper reported in her Los Angeles *Times* column the following day: "An irate citizen of Hollywood phoned to say....'I thought this was an honor that had to be earned.'" It's possible that the theatre was pressured into the Purdom ceremony. A Mann Theatres press release regarding the footprints in the late 1970s tells of a "story dating from the all-powerful studio days which says a big studio insisted one of their players had to be footprinted. The management [of the theatre] under terrific pressure finally bowed, but after a suitable time lapse the offending prints were quietly removed." There is also another possibility as to why his square disappeared without official explanation: an executive in the Fox West Coast Theatre organization decreed that Purdom should be removed on "moral grounds," as he had become romantically involved with Linda Christian, who at the time was married to Tyrone Power. The affair caused a considerable scandal. Today the space is occupied by Yul Brynner's square.

Since the Chinese Theatre's earliest years, many imprinting ceremonies have been planned, or at least contemplated, for such stars as Raquel Torres, Greta Garbo, Douglas Fairbanks, Jr., Chic Olsen and Ole Johnson, Lauren Bacall, Hedda Hopper, and Barbra Streisand. They never materialized.

Jean Hersholt makes shoe imprints for the Dionne Quintuplets.

Forecourt of the Stars